PARTICIPATION IN AMERICAN PRESIDENTIAL NOMINATIONS, 1976

PARTICIPATION IN AMERICAN PRESIDENTIAL NOMINATIONS, 1976

Austin Ranney

American Enterprise Institute for Public Policy Research
Washington, D.C.

Austin Ranney is a resident scholar of the American Enterprise Institute and a member of the Democratic National Committee's Commission on the Role and Future of Presidential Primaries.

ISBN 0-8447-3246-X

Library of Congress Catalog Card No. 77-76530

AEI Studies 149

Printed in the United States of America

CONTENTS

PARTICIPATION IN AMERICAN PRESIDENTIAL NOMINATIONS, 1976

1. The Development of Presidential Nominating Systems

The United States is the only democratic nation in the world that provides institutional mechanisms for widespread popular participation in the selection of party nominees for high elective office. Almost all of the major parties in the parliamentary democracies of western Europe, Scandinavia, the British Commonwealth, and Japan choose their national leaders—and consequently their candidates for prime minister—by votes, usually secret, of the parties' members holding seats in the national parliament. To be sure, most of these parties hold annual or biennial national conventions composed of delegates chosen by local and affiliated party organizations; but these conventions have no power to choose the parties' leaders.[1]

In the presidential democracies other than the United States (for example, Colombia, Costa Rica, and Venezuela), the parties' presidential candidates are indeed chosen by national delegate conventions, which superficially resemble those of the United States. However, the delegates to these conventions either are chosen by small numbers of

I am grateful to Leon Epstein, Evron Kirkpatrick, Jeane Kirkpatrick, and Byron Shafer, who read and made useful comments on an early draft of this paper.

[1] Canada is the principal exception to this rule. From 1867 to 1919 Canadian parties chose their national leaders, as British parties did, by votes of their parliamentary members. In 1919, however, the Canadian parties began selecting their leaders in national delegate conventions chosen and organized in a fashion similar, though not identical, to that of American conventions. They have done so ever since. See Carl Baar and Ellen Baar, "Party and Convention Organization and Leadership Selection in Canada and the United States," in Donald R. Matthews, ed., *Perspectives on Presidential Selection* (Washington, D.C.: The Brookings Institution, 1973), pp. 49-84.

enrolled, dues-paying members of regional and subregional party organizations, the most common form of selection; or they are ex officio delegates who receive their seats by virtue of the offices they hold (for example, all cabinet officers, all candidates for congress, and all candidates for other elective national offices). No delegates are elected by any form of presidential primary, and none are selected by local party caucuses or conventions open to any and all party *voters* (as opposed to dues-paying members).[2]

The development of presidential nominating systems in the United States has featured a succession of different systems. Each system in turn enjoyed a period of general acceptance, followed by accelerating protests that the nominations were being controlled undemocratically by secret meetings of small and unrepresentative cabals or irresponsible bosses. The remedy in each case was the adoption of a new system intended, above all, to open up the nomination process to greater popular participation. The three main systems in this succession were the congressional caucus, in force from 1800 to 1824; national conventions chosen by state party conventions, from 1832 to 1904; and national conventions chosen by a mix of direct primaries and state party conventions and committees, from 1904 to 1976.[3]

The Congressional Caucus, 1800–24. By 1800 both Jefferson's Republican party and Hamilton's Federalist party had developed fully organized congressional caucuses—that is, regular meetings of the party's members of Congress. In 1800 each party's caucus decided to recommend—that is, nominate—what we would call a national party ticket (Jefferson and Aaron Burr for the Republicans, John Adams and Charles Cotesworth Pinckney for the Federalists) to those party members who would become members of the Electoral College. This continued to be the dominant presidential nominating system until 1824, when it collapsed under three separate but cumulative pressures. The first was the likelihood that the caucus of the Republicans (by then the only party) would pass over Andrew Jackson, John Quincy Adams, Henry Clay, and John C. Calhoun in favor of William H. Crawford. The four prospective losers decided to discredit Crawford's

---

[2] The most comprehensive review of nominating processes in Western democracies is Leon D. Epstein, *Political Parties in Western Democracies* (New York: Frederick A. Praeger, 1967), chapters 7-8.

[3] More detailed accounts are given in Austin Ranney, *Curing the Mischiefs of Faction: Party Reform in America* (Berkeley: University of California Press, 1975), pp. 62-74, 121-126; and Paul T. David, Ralph M. Goldman, and Richard C. Bain, *The Politics of National Party Conventions* (Washington, D.C.: The Brookings Institution, 1960), chapter 2.

selection by attacking the legitimacy of the caucus system itself. The second was the growing insistence of state and local party leaders that they, not a small band of national leaders, should make presidential nominations. And the third was the rapid acceptance of the principal theme of Jacksonian democracy—the doctrine that ordinary Americans should participate as widely as possible in all governmental processes, including presidential nominations. Though the Republican caucus met in early 1824 and nominated Crawford, its recommendation was widely ignored by other party leaders, and Crawford finished well down the list in the 1824 election. Since then no congressional caucus has attempted to make a presidential nomination. After a brief transitional period, presidential candidates came to be nominated by the new institution of national conventions composed of delegates from the states.

National Conventions Chosen by State Party Organizations, 1832–1904. The first presidential nomination by a national convention composed of delegates chosen by state and local party organizations was made by the short-lived Anti-Masonic party in 1830. The two major parties of the emerging "second party system" soon followed suit, the National Republicans (Whigs) in 1831 and the Democratic Republicans (Democrats) in 1832. When the new Republican party was founded in 1854, it adopted as a matter of course the convention system, which was by then solidly established in the two older parties.

Although the organization and conduct of these conventions changed in certain respects, the features of greatest relevance for this paper remained the same until the first years of the twentieth century. The procedures for selecting delegates to the national conventions were determined almost entirely by rules the state parties made for themselves, not by public laws.[4] Under these rules each national convention decided how many votes each state delegation would have in the next convention, but left it up to each state party to decide for itself how its delegates would be chosen. The state parties chose a great variety of methods: some, for example, allowed the governor to choose the entire delegation, while others left the choice to the state central committee. The system most widely used, however, was the empowering of members of state conventions (them-

---

[4] In the 1870s and 1880s a number of states adopted laws regulating the conduct of certain party affairs, but no special provisions were made for the selection of national convention delegates: see Joseph R. Starr, "The Legal Status of American Political Parties," *American Political Science Review*, vol. 34 (June-August, 1940), pp. 439-455, 695-699.

selves chosen by party members in precinct and county caucuses and conventions) to select the delegates to the national conventions.

This structuring of the national nominating convention persisted essentially unchanged until 1904. Since then it has undergone several major changes, all inspired by a desire to maximize popular participation by ordinary party members (that is, registrants and ticket-voters) in the selection of presidential candidates. The first change was the application to presidential politics of the most radical reform ever made in the American (or any other) party system: the direct primary.

National Conventions Chosen by a Mix of Direct Primaries and State Party Conventions and Committees, 1904–76. The term direct primary is used in somewhat different senses by different people. In this paper it refers to a system in which (1) the parties' nominees to public office are chosen directly by rank-and-file party members rather than indirectly by their representatives in caucuses and conventions; and (2) they are chosen by primary elections—that is, elections administered by *public* authorities (not party authorities) using virtually the same *statutory* rules (not party rules) for printing, distributing, casting, and counting ballots that are used in general elections.

So defined, the first presidential primary law was enacted by Florida in 1904. It authorized any party to choose some or all of its delegates to the national convention by direct primary if it chose to do so (and Florida Democrats did so choose in 1904). In 1905 Wisconsin enacted a law requiring the direct election of *all* national-convention delegates of both parties. It also added the feature of a presidential preference poll through which the voters could directly express their preferences among the aspirants for their party's presidential nomination; the poll's results would guide the delegates' votes for the nomination at the national convention. By 1912 a total of fourteen states had some kind of presidential primary,[5] and in 1916 the total rose to twenty-six states.

After World War II, several states abandoned their presidential primaries, and by 1968 the number appeared to have stabilized at sixteen states plus the District of Columbia. These states (here and elsewhere in this paper the District of Columbia is counted as a state

---

[5] From their beginnings to the present there have been many variations in the forms of presidential primaries adopted by the various states. We shall consider the nature and consequences of some of the main variations later in this paper, but for the present it is necessary to use the blanket phrase "some kind of presidential primary."

for purposes of nominating and electing a President) and the years in which they held presidential primaries up to 1968 are as follows:[6]

> Alabama (1924–34, 1940–68)
> California (1912–68)
> District of Columbia (1956-68)
> Florida (1904–68; but only Democrats until 1956)
> Illinois (1912–68)
> Indiana (1912–68)
> Massachusetts (1912–68)
> Nebraska (1912–68)
> New Hampshire (1916–68)
> New Jersey (1912–68)
> New York (1912–68)
> Ohio (1916–68)
> Oregon (1912–68)
> Pennsylvania (1912–68)
> South Dakota (1912–68)
> West Virginia (1916–68)
> Wisconsin (1908–68)

Since 1968 the number of states holding presidential primaries has increased far more rapidly than at any time since the formative period from 1904 to 1916. Between 1968 and 1972 six states (Maryland, Michigan, New Mexico, North Carolina, Rhode Island, and Tennessee) adopted presidential primaries. Between 1972 and 1976 New Mexico repealed its primary, but seven more states (Georgia, Idaho, Kentucky, Montana, Nevada, Texas, and Vermont) added primaries. And Arkansas converted its optional primary, which had been on the books but not used in 1972, into a compulsory process which was used in 1976. The result of these changes has been a vertiginous rise since 1968 in the number and total population of states holding presidential primaries. The seventeen primary states of 1968 combined had 56 percent of the nation's estimated voting-age population. The thirty primary states of 1976 combined had 78 percent of the voting-age population. Even more important was the rise in the proportion of delegates chosen or bound by primaries, as shown in Table 1.

Three motives seem to have been most influential in bringing about the great proliferation of presidential primaries between 1968

---

[6] The most complete account of the waxing and waning of presidential primaries from 1904 to 1968 is James W. Davis, *Presidential Primaries: Road to the White House* (New York: Thomas Y. Crowell, 1967).

Table 1

PROLIFERATION OF PRESIDENTIAL PRIMARIES, 1968–76

Party and Coverage	1968	1972	1976
Democratic Party			
Number of states using a primary for selecting or binding national convention delegates	17	23	29[a]
Number of votes cast by delegates chosen or bound by primaries	983	1,862	2,183
Percent of all votes cast by delegates chosen or bound by primaries	37.5	60.5	72.6
Republican Party			
Number of states using a primary for selecting or binding national convention delegates	16	22	28[a]
Number of votes cast by delegates chosen or bound by primaries	458	710	1,533
Percent of all votes cast by delegates chosen or bound by primaries	34.3	52.7	67.9

[a] Does not include Vermont, which held a nonbinding presidential-preference poll but chose all delegates of both parties by caucuses and conventions.

Source: The primary laws of each state, including the proportion of each party's delegates chosen or bound by primaries, are summarized by Rhodes Cook in the *Congressional Quarterly Weekly Report,* January 21, 1976, pp. 225-242.

and 1976. The first was the judgment by party leaders in a number of states that the surest and least damaging way to comply with the new rules of the national Democratic party for choosing national convention delegates was to adopt a presidential primary and thereby segregate presidential politics from the state parties' many other activities. The second motive was a variant of the first: the calculation by many Democratic leaders that it would be easier to keep their states' delegations from being captured by "kooks" of the left or right if delegates were chosen by primaries instead of by the "participatory conventions" dictated by the new party rules. And wherever the Democrats succeeded in passing a state law establishing a primary election, that law usually, though not always, applied to the Republicans as well.

The third motive is more central to the concerns of this paper: the conviction shared by important segments of the states' political influentials that popular participation in presidential nominations should be greatly increased and that the best way to accomplish this goal is by adopting presidential primaries.

This paper has two main purposes. The first is to examine the doctrine of popular participation in presidential nominations. The second is to identify and explain the varying degrees to which the fifty states and the District of Columbia achieved such participation through their primaries and caucuses in 1976. We begin by exploring the basic idea of participation in nominations.

2. The Doctrine of Popular Participation in Nominations

Most politicians and many political analysts have long known that the nominating process plays a critical role in all democratic systems of selecting public leaders. General elections, to be sure, give the final answer to the question, Who shall rule? But nominations frame the question and thereby profoundly shape the answer. It seems clear, for example, that the processes by which the Democrats in 1976 decided that their nominee would be Jimmy Carter rather than Henry Jackson or Morris Udall or George Wallace and the Republicans decided theirs would be Gerald Ford rather than Ronald Reagan were more important for deciding the *kind* of person who would occupy the White House for the next four years than was the process by which the voters in November chose between Carter and Ford.

It is not surprising that disputes about the proper organization and role of political parties—disputes that have divided Americans so often since the earliest days of the Republic—have centered more on how nominations should be made than on any other issue.[7] The recent controversies over a uniform national presidential primary and over the rules adopted by the McGovern-Fraser and Mikulski commissions, like the controversies over the congressional caucus a century and a half earlier, turn mainly on the two fundamental questions: *Who should participate* in making presidential nominations? And *how directly* should they participate? We turn now to a brief review of the main positions put forth on each issue.

Who Should Participate? From the decades of discussions, three main positions have emerged on the issue of who should participate in making presidential nominations.

---

[7] See Ranney, *Mischiefs of Faction*; M. I. Ostrogorski, *Democracy and the Organization of Political Parties,* translated from the French by Frederick Clarke (New York: Macmillan, 1902), vol. II; and Frederick W. Dallinger, *Nominations for Elective Office in the United States* (New York: Longmans, Green, 1897).

(1) Party regulars. The most restrictive position of the three, in that it would confine participation to the smallest proportion of the population, holds that presidential nominations should be made by people with a strong and continuous involvement in and commitment to the party in whose name the nomination is made. That is, people should *earn* the right to help select their party presidential nominees; they should earn it by service to their party and by establishing their bona fides as good party soldiers who can be counted on to support the party's ticket even if their own choices for candidate and platform stands do not prevail.

The classical statement of this position was made by the political scientist E. E. Schattschneider, who argued that a sharp distinction should always be made between a party's *supporters* (those who regularly vote for its nominees but do nothing else to promote its cause) and its *members* (those who are continuously active in all its affairs). He continued:

> If the party is described as a political enterprise conducted by a group of working politicians *supported* by partisan voters who approve of the party but are merely partisans (not members of a fictitious association), the parties would seem less wicked. . . . Will the parties be less responsive to the needs of the voters if their private character is generally recognized? Probably not. The parties do not need laws to make them sensitive to the wishes of the voters any more than we need laws compelling merchants to please their customers. The sovereignty of the voter consists in his freedom of choice just as the sovereignty of the consumer in the economic system consists in his freedom to trade in a competitive market. This is enough; little can be added to it by inventing an imaginary membership in a fictitious party association. Democracy is not to be found *in* the parties but *between* the parties.[8]

In the same vein, Schattschneider argued that parties do their nominating job best if the party regulars pick the candidates. After all, the regulars' main object is to win elections, and that means they will prefer the candidates most likely to appeal to the largest numbers of voters. That outlook, in turn, makes for parties that are not only strong and responsive but also moderate and constantly seeking the combination of people and programs that will have the greatest voter appeal. For purely selfish reasons, then, they are forced to search for

---

[8] E. E. Schattschneider, *Party Government* (New York: Farrar and Rinehart, 1940), pp. 59-60, italics in the original.

compromise and consensus that will unite the nation rather than contribute to sharp ideological cleavages that will divide it.

From Schattschneider's point of view the old congressional caucus was an excellent mechanism for making presidential nominations, though it is admittedly gone forever.[9] The pre-reform national conventions (those held before 1972) were also very good for the same purposes,[10] and even the pre-1972 mix of primaries, caucuses, and conventions worked very well.[11]

Whatever may be its merits, however, the party-regulars position has lost considerable ground in recent years to two less restrictive notions.

(2) Issue and candidate enthusiasts. Between 1968 and 1973 the Democratic party established two reform commissions to draw up new rules governing the selection of delegates to Democratic national conventions.[12] Both commissions based their recommendations on strongly held views of who should participate in choosing convention delegates and presidential nominees. They rejected the idea that past service to the party and anticipated service to the party should constitute a qualification or even an advantage for choosing or becoming delegates. The basic criterion, both commissions believed, should be a person's enthusiasm for a particular issue position or a particular candidate *in the year of the convention.* The critical question is not what has the would-be participant done for the party, but how much does he or she want to advance the cause of a particular candidate or policy position in the party's councils.

The commissions believed that this view of who should participate would, if implemented by properly drawn and scrupulously enforced rules, make the nominating process far more democratic than that provided by the old, discredited process dominated by party regulars. It would guarantee that more people would participate, and that in itself would be a major gain for democracy. In addition, it would

---

[9] Ibid., pp. 152-153.

[10] See Aaron B. Wildavsky, "On the Superiority of National Conventions," *Review of Politics*, vol. 24 (July 1962), pp. 307-319; and Herbert McClosky, "Are Political Conventions Undemocratic?" *New York Times Magazine*, August 4, 1968, pp. 15-21.

[11] Nelson W. Polsby and Aaron B. Wildavsky, *Presidential Elections*, 4th ed. (New York: Charles Scribner's Sons, 1976), pp. 220-237; and Hugh A. Bone, *American Politics and the Party System*, 4th ed. (New York: McGraw-Hill Book Company, 1971), pp. 313-321.

[12] The two commissions are generally referred to by the names of their chairpersons: the McGovern-Fraser commission, 1969-72, and the Mikulski commission, 1973-76.

guarantee that the convention's platform and nominee would be far more in accord than ever before with the issue and candidate preferences of active Democrats.

Thus, the report of the first (McGovern-Fraser) commission stated that one of the worst features of the 1968 convention was the fact that

> more than a third of the Convention delegates had, in effect, already been selected prior to 1968—before either the major issues or the possible presidential candidates were known. By the time President Johnson announced his withdrawal from the nominating contest, the delegates selection process had begun in all but twelve states.[13]

To prevent any repetition of such a state of affairs, the Mikulski commission's rules governing delegate selection for the 1976 Democratic national convention provided that "all steps in the delegate selection process . . . must take place within the calendar year of the Democratic National Convention . . ." (Rule 3-A); that delegates be chosen "in a manner which fairly reflects the division of preferences expressed by those who participate in the presidential nominating process" (Rule 11); and that "no person shall serve as an automatic or ex officio voting delegate at any level of the delegate selection process by virtue of holding a public or party office" (Rule 13).[14]

Since people who occasionally become enthusiastic for a particular candidate or policy far outnumber those who work for a party year-in and year-out through many changes of issue and candidate contests, this second view of who should participate is clearly less restrictive of participation than the party-regulars view. But both views are more restrictive than the third, which underlies all direct primaries and which in recent years has dominated the presidential nominating process more and more.

(3) Ordinary voters. Each of the first national conventions of 1831–32 and every convention since has been a kind of representative assembly, for each has been composed of delegates selected by party members (variously defined) for the *indirect* expression of the members' preferences for candidates and platforms. And, as we shall see, the conventions have been subject to the problems and criticisms that beset all representative institutions.

---

[13] *Mandate for Reform* (Washington, D.C.: Democratic National Committee, 1970), p. 10.

[14] *Democrats All*, mimeo. (Washington, D.C.: Democratic National Committee, 1973), pp. 15-24.

Like the reforms of the McGovern-Fraser and Mikulski commissions, the presidential primaries adopted by various states since 1904 have not been intended to replace the conventions entirely. Rather, their purpose has been to make the conventions responsive to ordinary voters' desires. This could be done best, in the view of advocates of primaries, by having the voters choose the delegates. Thus the delegates would be chosen by and responsive to, not a handful of party regulars or a few thousand issue/candidate enthusiasts, but millions of ordinary voters.

But *which* ordinary voters? Two distinct answers to this question have emerged; one has been institutionalized in "closed primaries," the other in "crossover primaries." Of the thirty states holding presidential primaries in 1976, fifteen used closed primaries.[15] In each of these states every voter was required to register as a Democrat, Republican, Independent, or member of some third party. Registration closed from nine to thirty-eight days prior to primary-election day, and during this period voters could not change their party registrations. On primary-election day only a voter registered as a member of a particular party was legally eligible to vote in that party's primary (though in New Hampshire registered Independents could vote in whichever primary they chose).

The other fifteen states held one or the other of two types of crossover primaries. Montana and Wisconsin held completely open primaries: in each state there was prior voter registration, but party preference was not asked or recorded. On primary day, each registered voter took the ballots of *both* parties into the booth, marked whichever he desired, and discarded the other. The remaining thirteen crossover states [16] also had prior registration with no recorded party affiliation. On primary day each voter received whichever ballot he publicly requested from the election officials at the polls. But in all fifteen states the key point was that the primary laws provided no devices for keeping Republicans from voting in Democratic primaries or Democrats from voting in Republican primaries. That is why all fifteen, despite their differences in other respects, were generally called crossover states.

The crossover system is, of course, the least restrictive of the present forms of participation in selecting national convention dele-

---

[15] The closed-primary states were California, the District of Columbia, Florida, Kentucky, Maryland, Massachusetts, Nebraska, Nevada, New Hampshire, New York, North Carolina, Oregon, Pennsylvania, South Dakota, and West Virginia.

[16] In addition to Montana and Wisconsin, the crossover-primary states were Alabama, Arkansas, Georgia, Idaho, Illinois, Indiana, Michigan, New Jersey, Ohio, Rhode Island, Tennessee, Texas, and Vermont.

gates. It would seem to violate the Democrats' Rule 2 that "state parties must take all feasible steps to restrict participation in the delegate selection process to Democratic voters only," though the party's Compliance Review Commission, at the very last minute, held otherwise. But even in the closed primaries a Democrat is anyone who claims to be one, and it seems highly unlikely that significantly more demanding qualifications will ever be required of ordinary voters who want to participate in choosing national convention delegates.

How Free Should the Delegates Be? We noted earlier that the parties' national nominating conventions are representative assemblies and, as such, face the same theoretical issues and practical problems faced by all representative institutions. One example is the much-discussed dilemma as to whether representatives should be restricted to voting only for those persons and measures their constituents are known to favor or left free to exercise their own best judgment and then be held accountable for their conduct. The problem is even more complex in national party conventions than in most representative assemblies, for convention delegates' terms of office are only a few days, not two or four years; delegates do not run for reelection in the ordinary sense of the term, and thus they are not accountable in the sense that the members of most representative assemblies are.

Discussions of this issue usually turn on two classical opposing views. The best-known exponent of one is Edmund Burke, who argued that representatives are in a better position than their constituents to make informed judgments on most matters, and so they should be true representatives, not rubber stamps. The other, often associated with Jean Jacques Rousseau, holds that representatives should be *only* agents of their constituents—merely conduits for carrying the constituents' views to the representative assembly. The Rousseau view has had a good deal of impact on the parties' rules. For example, one of the Democrats' rules requires that at all stages of the selection process the presidential preference of anyone running for national convention delegate must be made clear (Rule 10-A). Another requires that all candidates for delegate "allocated to or identified with Presidential candidates shall be subject to the approval of said candidate" (Rule 10-B)—presumably to ensure the delegates' suitability and loyalty to the presidential candidates they say they favor. The Republicans adopted an even stronger version of the Rousseau position. Prior to their 1976 convention there was apprehension among the Ford forces that some delegates nominally bound to vote for Ford by state law would follow their own personal preferences and vote for Reagan instead; so the Ford-dominated Rules Committee proposed, and the convention adopted, the "justice resolution" (Rule 18), which required all delegates elected in primary states to vote according to the laws of their states—that is, to vote at the convention for the candidate they were pledged to support on the primary ballot.[17]

There is, be it noted, considerable variation in how closely state primary laws bind delegates to vote for particular candidates. The most common rule, which obtains in seventeen states, provides that delegates in both parties are bound by the results of the presidential preference poll.[18] In six states either there is no preference poll or its results are only advisory, but the delegates in both parties are legally bound to vote at the convention for the candidate for whom they expressed a preference when they were running for their delegate posts.[19] In three states the delegates of one party are bound, but those of the other party are free to vote as they wish.[20] And in four states the delegates of both parties are entirely free to vote as they wish.[21] Accordingly, the state primary laws for the most part reflect the commitment to the Rousseau position manifest in the party rules; even so, in nearly a quarter of the states the delegates are legally free of any instructions by those who elect them.

The Goals of Popular Participation. The foregoing makes clear that both the Democratic party's reform rules and the recent proliferation of state presidential primaries are intended to increase greatly the amount of popular participation in the selection of national convention delegates and therefore in the choosing of presidential candidates. But to what end? The party reformers and state legislators who have pressed for these changes have done so in part because of their adherence, explicit or implicit, to a powerful body of ideas known to political theorists as the doctrine of participatory democracy.[22]

---

[17] *Congressional Quarterly Weekly Report*, August 21, 1976, p. 2255.

[18] Arkansas, California, the District of Columbia, Florida, Georgia, Idaho, Indiana, Kentucky, Massachusetts, Michigan, Nevada, North Carolina, Oregon, Rhode Island, South Dakota, Tennessee, and Wisconsin. In Georgia, Democratic delegates are bound by the presidential preference poll, but Republican delegates are bound only by their own stated preferences.

[19] Alabama, Illinois, Nebraska, New Hampshire, New Jersey, and Texas.

[20] Maryland (Republicans only are bound), Pennsylvania (Democrats only), and Montana (Democrats only).

[21] New York, Ohio, Vermont, and West Virginia.

[22] Among the more useful recent general expositions of this doctrine are: Carole Pateman, *Participation and Democratic Theory* (Cambridge, England: Cambridge University Press, 1970); Peter Bachrach, *The Theory of Democratic Elitism: A Critique* (Boston: Little, Brown, 1967); and Terence E. Cook and Patrick M. Morgan, *Participatory Democracy* (San Francisco: Canfield Press, 1971).

According to their application of this doctrine, the principal anticipated benefits of a more participatory nominating process are the following:

(1) More representative conventions. The reasoning is simple: the greater the popular participation in choosing delegates, the more the delegates chosen are likely to transmit accurately the candidate and platform preferences of the rank and file.

(2) More legitimate conventions and candidates. The greater the popular participation and the more representative the results, the greater will be the legitimacy of the whole convention process and the tickets it produces in the eyes of the citizens.

(3) More public support of the political system. In recent years many America-watchers have become concerned about what they believe to be a growing cynicism toward and distrust of America's political institutions, especially the party system. Greater participation in presidential nominations will help turn this around, it is argued; for the more the people feel that the presidential nominating system is legitimate and that they have a real voice in it, the more likely they are to have faith in the parties, the elections, and the entire political system. The McGovern-Fraser commission's final report in 1970 expressed this view very well:

> We view popular participation as the lifeblood of the National Convention. . . . We believe that popular participation is more than a proud heritage of our party, more even than a first principle. We believe that popular control of the Democratic Party is necessary for its survival. . . . If we are not an open party, if we do not represent the demands of change, then the danger is not that people will go to the Republican Party; it is that there will no longer be a way for people committed to orderly change to fulfill their needs and desires within our traditional political system. It is that they will turn to third and fourth party politics or the anti-politics of the street.[23]

The triumph of this point of view gave the American people in 1976 a far greater opportunity than ever before to participate in the selection of national convention delegates and in the choice of the two parties' candidates for President. I turn now to a description and analysis of how many voters used that opportunity.

---

[23] *Mandate for Reform,* pp. 33, 49.

14

3. Participation in the 1976 Presidential Nominations

Participation in Precinct Caucuses. We noted earlier that the main thrust of the 1969 McGovern-Fraser rules and their 1973 revision by the Mikulski commission was to open up participation in party affairs to all Democrats who wanted to participate and to strip the party regulars of any special advantage they might previously have enjoyed. In 1976 by far the most common form of participation was voting in primaries, which were held in thirty of the fifty-one states (including the District of Columbia). Accordingly, most of this paper focuses on voting in the primaries. But we should not overlook the fact that twenty-one states, with a combined voting-age population of 33,389,000 (22.2 percent of the national voting-age population) chose their national convention delegates by processes that began with caucuses of (self-designated) party members in the precincts and ended with state conventions selecting delegates to the national convention.

To keep a check on how many people participated in this manner, *Congressional Quarterly* collected reports from Democratic state party organizations (no data for the Republicans were gathered) estimating the numbers of people who participated in the first-round precinct caucuses. These reports are, at best, only approximations, for they depend upon the diligence and accuracy of local as well as state party officials, and there is reason to believe that some inflated the numbers to make their organizations look good. Nevertheless, their reports are the best data we have or are likely to get. And, as summarized in Table 2, they show how much less participation there was in the participatory caucuses than in the primaries.

The mean proportion of the voting-age population attending the caucuses in the twenty-one states was 1.9 percent, while the mean proportion of the voting-age population voting in Democratic primaries in the closed-primary states (the best direct comparison we can make with the caucus states) was 18.6 percent—nearly ten times higher. Or again, the highest caucus turnout, according to *Congressional Quarterly*, came in Connecticut, where the 106,000 persons reported as attending constituted about 19 percent of the state's registered Democrats.[24] By contrast, in California, the state with the highest turnout of registered voters in the primary elections (see Table 3), 71.7 percent of the registered Democrats voted in their primary.

---

[24] *Congressional Quarterly Weekly Report*, July 10, 1976, p. 1809.

Table 2

ESTIMATED PARTICIPATION IN DEMOCRATIC FIRST-LEVEL PRECINCT CAUCUSES FOR NATIONAL DELEGATE SELECTION, NONPRIMARY STATES, 1976

State	Estimated Voting-Age Population	Attendance at Precinct Caucuses	
		Estimated number of persons	Percent of voting-age population
Alaska	231,000	1,000	0.4
Arizona	1,555,000	26,700	1.7
Colorado	1,773,000	30,000	1.7
Connecticut	2,211,000	106,600	4.8
Hawaii	600,000	3,000	0.5
Iowa	2,010,000	45,000	2.2
Kansas	1,610,000	N.A.	—
Louisiana	2,532,000	120,000	4.7
Maine	741,000	6,500	0.9
Minnesota	2,721,000	58,000	2.1
Mississippi	1,544,000	60,000	3.9
Missouri	3,348,000	20,000	0.6
New Mexico	771,000	10,000	1.3
North Dakota	432,000	3,000	0.7
Oklahoma	1,937,000	65,000	3.3
South Carolina	1,933,000	63,000	3.2
Utah	783,000	16,300	2.1
Vermont	327,000	2,500	0.8
Virginia	3,528,000	20,000	0.6
Washington	2,536,000	60,000	2.4
Wyoming	266,000	600	0.2

Source: Voting-age population for the states is taken from Bureau of the Census, *Population Estimates and Projections*, Series P-25, no. 626, issued May 1976. Attendance at the Democratic precinct caucuses is taken from estimates given to *Congressional Quarterly* by Democratic state chairmen and reported in various issues of *Congressional Quarterly Weekly Report* from January 24, 1976, to May 15, 1976.

In short, no matter how much more open and participatory the local caucuses of 1976 may have been than those in any previous year, they attracted far less actual participation than the direct primaries.

Measures of Voting Turnout in Primaries. Political scientists have long been concerned with measuring levels of popular participation in political affairs, and a number of typologies of participation have been developed.[25] For most people the sole form of political participation is voting in official elections, including primary elections. Hence political scientists have made more studies of voting and non-voting elections than of any other form of participation.[26]

In the course of these studies three main measures of the degree of participation, or voting turnout, have been developed:

(1) Based on voting-age population (VAP). Most studies of voting turnout[27] use a simple measure:

$$\text{voting turnout} = \frac{\text{number of votes cast}}{\text{voting-age population}}$$

This measure has a number of advantages, which do much to account for its widespread use. First, the data are easily obtained. Official election returns for both primary and general elections for President, governor, U.S. senator, and U.S. representative, have been collected, verified, and published in a series of authoritative volumes edited by Richard Scammon.[28] The denominator for the formula has been provided since 1960 by estimates of the number of persons in each state who achieved the minimum voting age or more by the first day of November, issued periodically by the Bureau of the Census.[29]

Not only does this measure permit the use of the most easily obtained information, but also it allows analysts to include in their calculations the two states, Ohio and Wisconsin, which do not require or maintain any statewide summary of the number of registered voters.

However, the measure also has several disadvantages. In particular, the VAP base exaggerates the potential electorate and therefore makes turnout figures lower than they should be. The Bureau of the Census includes all persons of voting age, including a number who are legally ineligible to vote—aliens, inmates of penal institu-

---

[25] See Lester W. Milbrath, *Political Participation* (Skokie, Ill.: Rand McNally, 1965), chap. 1.

[26] The first major study was Charles E. Merriam and Harold F. Gosnell, *Non-Voting* (Chicago: University of Chicago Press, 1924).

[27] See, for example, *Report of the President's Commission on Registration and Voting Participation* (Washington, D.C.: November 1963).

[28] Richard M. Scammon, ed., *America Votes* (Washington, D.C.: Elections Research Center and Congressional Quarterly), 11 volumes to date.

[29] The most recent example is Bureau of the Census, *Population Estimates and Projections*, Series P-25, no. 626, issued May 1976.

tions, ex-convicts, and others. The measure also makes no allowance for the considerable variations in difficulty in the registration laws of the various states and their impact on differences in voting turnout.[30] Accordingly, some scholars prefer a second measure.

(2) Based on registered voters (RV). This measure, too, has a simple formula:

$$\text{voting turnout} = \frac{\text{number of votes cast in a given election}}{\text{number of registered voters eligible for that election}}$$

The RV measure has several advantages. The denominator is the true *legal* potential electorate; hence it provides a more accurate picture than the VAP measure of how many of the people who could have voted actually did. By largely eliminating the problems caused by variations in registration laws, it provides a much truer comparison with turnout rates in European nations. In addition, studies of turnout in primary elections, such as this one, are enabled (at least in all states with party registration) to focus on each party's primary and see if there are significant differences between the parties.[31]

(3) Reported voting in sample surveys. Just about every sample survey of the American electorate keyed to a particular election asks its respondents whether or not they voted in that election, and their replies provide a third measure of turnout. The turnout figure produced by taking the proportion of self-reported voters to self-reported nonvoters, however, is almost invariably much higher than that produced by either the RV or VAP measures—presumably because some respondents in every sample claim to have voted when they did not. In addition, most national surveys, such as those made by the Center for Political Studies at the University of Michigan, study *national* samples, not fifty-one state samples; and the technical requirements of sampling make it impossible for them to give reports on turnout or anything else for particular states. The only exception to this rule is the series of surveys conducted by the Bureau of the Census biennially. The bureau polls samples in all fifty states and in the District of Columbia and thus its surveys permit state-by-state

---

[30] The point is well made in Steven J. Rosenstone and Raymond E. Wolfinger, "The Effect of Registration Laws on Voter Turnout," a paper presented at the 1976 Annual Meeting of the American Political Science Association, The Palmer House, Chicago, Illinois, September 2-5, 1976.

[31] The point is made by William D. Morris and Otto A. Davis, "The Sport of Kings: Turnout in Presidential Preference Primaries," a paper presented at the 1975 Annual Meeting of the American Political Science Association, San Francisco Hilton Hotel, San Francisco, California, September 2-5, 1975.

analysis as well as national analysis. But neither the Michigan nor the Census surveys have as yet shown much interest in primary elections and so are of little use for the purposes of this study.

Differences between the VAP and RV Measures. Since the remainder of this paper seeks to describe and explain the differences among the states in presidential primary turnout in 1976, it is necessary to choose either the VAP or the RV base as the denominator for the measure of turnout.

The choice makes a significant difference, for one base is considerably more useful than the other for explaining variations in *primary* turnout (as distinguished from turnout in general). Bear in mind that the VAP base includes ineligible persons and eligible but unregistered persons as well as registered voters. In the twenty-six states that held primaries for both parties and kept complete state-wide registration and voting figures in 1976 (the District of Columbia, New York, Ohio, and Wisconsin did not), the percent of VAP registered prior to the primaries ranged from 81.5 (Vermont) to 46.7 (Nevada), with a mean of 67.8. Thus, on the average, about one-third of the potential voters were not registered for the primaries and could not have voted even if they had wanted to.

Most students of the American electoral system believe that the registration requirements in many of our states are major barriers to registration and therefore go far toward explaining the much-discussed fact that turnouts in American elections are generally much lower than those in other democratic nations.[32] If that is correct, we would expect RV turnout to be higher than VAP turnout in primaries as well as in general elections; and that was indeed the case in 1976. As Table 3 shows, the mean turnout in the 1976 presidential primaries was 42.9 percent if calculated on the RV base, but only 28.2 percent if the VAP base is used. Similar differences appear in general elections as well: for example, Census Bureau figures for the 1972 presidential general election show that the turnout was 55.7 percent of the VAP and 75.7 percent of the RVs.

It is clear, then, that registration is a significant barrier to voting in many American states, and interstate comparisons of voting turnout using the VAP base are bound to be strongly affected by the im-

[32] See Rosenstone and Wolfinger, "Effect of Registration Laws"; Stanley Kelley, Jr., Richard E. Ayres, and William G. Bowen, "Registration and Voting: Putting First Things First," *American Political Science Review*, vol. 61 (June 1967), pp. 359-379; and Jae-On Kim, John R. Petrocik, and Stephen N. Enokson, "Voter Turnout Among the American States: Systemic and Individual Components," *American Political Science Review*, vol. 69 (March 1975), pp. 107-131.

Table 3

TURNOUT OF VOTERS IN PRESIDENTIAL PRIMARIES, 1976

State	Total Votes Cast	Estimated VAP	Percent of VAP Voting	Total Registered Voters	Percent of RV Voting
Alabama	665,855	2,501,000	26.6	1,792,582	37.1
Arkansas	534,341	1,503,000	35.5	961,399	55.6
California	5,709,853	15,294,000	37.3	7,701,888	74.1
Florida	1,910,149	6,326,000	30.2	3,381,750	56.5
Georgia	690,843	3,375,000	30.5	2,090,267	33.0
Idaho	164,960	567,000	29.1	457,965	36.0
Illinois	2,087,807	7,718,000	27.0	5,753,155	36.3
Indiana	1,245,715	3,640,000	34.2	2,910,086	42.8
Kentucky	439,534	2,374,000	18.5	1,545,915	28.4
Maryland	757,717	2,863,000	26.5	1,679,126	45.1
Massachusetts	941,950	4,173,000	22.6	1,766,812	53.3
Michigan	1,771,480	6,268,000	28.3	4,575,335	38.7
Montana	196,620	518,000	37.9	411,090	47.8
Nebraska	395,390	1,080,000	36.6	736,567	53.7
Nevada	122,991	424,000	29.0	198,073	62.1
New Hampshire	187,312	574,000	32.6	319,880	58.6
New Jersey	602,961	5,514,000	11.7	3,511,364	17.2
North Carolina	798,559	3,847,000	20.7	2,265,048	35.2
Oregon	730,167	1,653,000	44.2	1,177,909	62.0
Pennsylvania	2,183,122	8,441,000	25.9	5,023,278	43.5
Rhode Island	74,700	648,000	11.5	514,334	14.5
South Dakota	142,748	469,000	30.4	366,856	38.9
Tennessee	574,359	2,958,000	19.4	1,899,593	30.2
Texas	1,979,001	8,503,000	23.3	5,360,434	36.9
Vermont	72,270	327,000	22.1	266,649	27.1
West Virginia	528,269	1,281,000	41.2	1,042,502	50.7
Ohio	2,083,207	7,459,000	27.9	no statewide registration	
Wisconsin	1,333,373	3,211,000	41.5	no statewide registration	
Total	28,925,253	103,149,000		57,709,858	
Mean turnout			28.2		42.9

Source: The data on registration and votes cast in the 1976 primaries were compiled by the Congressional Research Service of the Library of Congress and were furnished to the author by the courtesy of Carol F. Casey. The data on estimated voting-age population are from Bureau of Census, *Current Population Reports,* Series P-25, no. 626, issued May 1976.

pact of variations in registration requirements. Indeed, the correlation (Spearman's r_s) between the states' rankings on VAP turnout and on RV turnout in the 1976 primaries is .80—a high, but far from perfect, relationship.

The RV electorate, however, includes only persons who have already passed whatever barriers the states' registration laws may put in the way of voting. Thus, by using the RV base for interstate turnout comparisons, we can eliminate any distortions due to restrictive or facilitative registration laws and focus more clearly on the effects of such factors as primary laws, campaign spending, and closeness of the races than we could if we adopted the VAP base.

To illustrate: when we observe that the VAP turnout in California's 1976 presidential primary was 37.3 percent while Rhode Island's was only 11.5 percent, we might well surmise that the gap was produced mainly by California's facilitative registration laws and Rhode Island's restrictive ones. But when we also observe that the RV turnout was 74.1 percent for California and 14.5 percent for Rhode Island, knowing as we do that the latter two figures are percentages of persons who have already complied with their states' registration requirements however permissive or restrictive, we must search elsewhere for explanations of the differences in turnout between the two states.

In what follows, accordingly, I shall use the RV base as the denominator for the measure of turnout, except in a few instances in which the VAP base will be noted as more useful.

Turnout Rates in the 1976 Presidential Primaries. Thirty states held presidential primaries in 1976. Our purposes, however, require that four of them be omitted from the analysis. In New York no state-wide data were assembled or are now available for the number of persons who cast votes for national convention delegates in the state's complicated primary. In the District of Columbia, only the Democrats held a presidential primary, so the turnout was misleadingly low compared with that in the other states, all of which held primaries for both parties. Neither Ohio nor Wisconsin kept state-wide figures on the number of registered voters. These four states will be ignored in this discussion.

For each of the remaining twenty-six states, Table 3 shows the total votes cast in its presidential primary, the estimated voting-age population as of November 1, 1976, the turnout rate on the VAP basis, the total number of registered voters, and the turnout rate on the RV basis. The twenty-six states had a mean turnout rate of 42.9 percent on the RV basis and 27.6 percent on the VAP basis.

We should also note, however, that there was a considerable variation among the turnout rates of the various states. On the RV basis, the range was from California's high of 74.1 percent to Rhode Island's low of 14.5 percent, with a mean of 42.9 and a standard deviation of 13.94. These interstate variations constitute the principal phenomena we are trying to explain.

It is interesting to note that in 1972 twelve of these states also held formally contested presidential primaries (that is, more than one candidate was on the ballot for each party in each of the twelve states in both 1972 and 1976). The mean RV turnout for these states in 1972 was 46.7 percent. This was nearly four percentage points *higher* than in the same states in 1976 despite the fact that the 1972 Republican contests were token fights only while both parties' primaries were hotly contested in 1976.

One other comparison with earlier years may be of interest. In an article published in 1972, I reported on turnout in all competitive presidential primaries from 1948 through 1968, using the VAP measure and defining a competitive primary as one in which (a) two or more candidates or candidate-pledged slates appeared on each party's ballot, (b) at least one major national contender appeared on each party's ballot, and (c) in neither party did the winning candidate or slate get more than 80 percent of the votes. Only eleven primaries satisfied these criteria in the 1948–68 period (all of them falling in either 1952 or 1968), and their mean voting turnout was 39 percent.[33]

Using the same criteria, no 1972 primaries qualified as competitive; but in 1976 no less than twenty-two of the twenty-eight states (including Ohio and Wisconsin for this analysis) met the standards.[34] For those states the mean turnout, using the comparable VAP base, was 28 percent—a drop of eleven percentage points from the figure for the 1948–68 period.

Accordingly, while in 1976 the nation had far more presidential primaries—and far more closely contested ones—than ever before, there was a sharp drop-off in turnout. That drop, moreover, was larger than the much-discussed drop-off in turnout in presidential general elections. The highest VAP turnout in general elections in the 1948–68 period was 62.8 percent in 1960, which fell to 53.4 percent in the 1976 general election. This drop of 9.4 percentage points, con-

[33] Austin Ranney, "Turnout and Representation in Presidential Primary Elections," *American Political Science Review*, vol. 66 (March 1972), pp. 21-37.

[34] The following states were excluded: Georgia, where Carter got 83 percent of the votes in the Democratic primary; New Jersey and Pennsylvania, where only Ford was on the Republican ballot; and West Virginia, where Robert Byrd got 89 percent of the votes in the Democratic primary.

siderable though it is, is still lower than the eleven-point drop in turn-out in competitive presidential primaries in the same period.

The Two Parties Compared. As noted earlier, fifteen of the thirty state primary laws restricted voting to preregistered party members. For reasons already stated, we must exclude two of these, the District of Columbia and New York, from our analysis. The turnout of RVs for both parties in each of the remaining thirteen states is shown in Table 4. Table 4 shows that the mean turnouts for both parties were almost identical—50.3 percent for the Democrats, and 50.6 percent for the Republicans.

As is usually the case, however, these mean turnouts conceal substantial variations in turnout within each of the parties and sub-stantial disparities between the parties. For instance, the Democrats' greatest turnout margin over the Republicans was in Massachusetts (57.3 percent to 42.0 percent), where Reagan did not campaign and where the Democrats had a close fight, with Jackson edging Udall, Wallace, and Carter. The other big Democratic margin was in Penn-

Table 4

TURNOUT OF REGISTERED VOTERS, BY PARTY, IN CLOSED-PRIMARY STATES, 1976

State	Democrats			Republicans		
	Number regis-tered	Votes cast in primary	Percent of RVs voting	Number regis-tered	Votes cast in primary	Percent of RVs voting
California	4,701,736	3,373,732	71.7	3,000,152	2,336,121	77.9
Florida	2,380,954	1,300,330	54.6	1,000,796	609,819	60.9
Kentucky	1,077,360	306,006	28.4	468,555	133,528	28.5
Maryland	1,240,042	591,746	47.7	439,084	165,971	37.8
Massachusetts	1,305,863	747,634	57.3	460,949	193,411	42.0
Nebraska	358,702	181,910	50.7	377,865	213,480	56.5
Nevada	125,705	75,242	59.9	72,368	47,749	66.0
New Hampshire	142,665	75,638	53.0	177,215	111,674	63.0
North Carolina	1,708,048	604,832	35.4	557,000	193,727	34.8
Oregon	714,917	432,632	60.5	462,992	297,535	64.3
Pennsylvania	2,801,649	1,385,042	49.4	2,221,629	796,660	35.9
South Dakota	177,459	58,671	33.1	189,397	84,077	44.4
West Virginia	705,062	372,577	52.8	337,440	155,692	46.1
Mean turnout			50.3			50.6

Source: Same as for Table 3.

sylvania (49.4 percent to 35.9 percent) where Ford was the only candidate on the Republican ballot and where the Democratic race was billed by the news media as Jackson's last stand against Carter (indeed, Jackson did drop out after losing this race to Carter). The Republicans' biggest turnout edges over the Democrats came in South Dakota (44.9 percent to 33.1 percent) and New Hampshire (63.0 percent to 53.0 percent); both states had close Ford-Reagan contests, but the Democrats had hot contests as well. Thus, it seems that closeness of competition is not the sole cause of high primary turnouts. We shall return to this point later.

Primary–General Election Differentials in 1976. One of the most persistent features of American elections is the fact that turnout in primary elections is almost invariably much lower than that in the ensuing general elections for the same offices. For example, my data show that the mean VAP turnout in primary elections for governor in the period 1962–72 was 29.8 percent compared to a mean turnout of 52.5 in the ensuing general elections; for U.S. senators the mean turnout in primary elections was 24.5 percent compared with a mean turnout in the general elections of 51.0 percent.[35]

The 1972 study mentioned earlier showed that the seventy-two presidential primaries between 1948 and 1968 produced a mean VAP turnout of 27 percent compared with a mean VAP turnout of 62 percent in the ensuing general elections—an increase of thirty-five percentage points from the primary to the general election. For the eleven competitive primaries, the mean VAP turnout was 39 percent and the mean VAP turnout in the ensuing general elections was 69 percent— an increase of thirty points from primary to general elections.

In 1976, as we have seen, twenty-two of the twenty-six states listed in Table 3 satisfied the criteria for having competitive presidential primaries. Their VAP turnouts in the primaries and general election are shown in Table 5. The figures in Table 5 show that the mean VAP turnout in the 1976 competitive primaries was 28.9 percent, while the mean VAP turnout in those states in the general election was 53.3 percent. Thus both the primary and general-election turnout figures were substantially lower in 1976 than in the 1948–68 period, while the increase from the primary to the general election also fell to 24.4 percentage points. Even so, the established turnout rule continues to hold: turnout in primary elections is generally about

---

[35] Austin Ranney, "Parties in State Politics," in Herbert Jacob and Kenneth N. Vines, eds., *Politics in the American States*, 3rd ed. (Boston: Little, Brown and Company, 1976), Table 1.

Table 5

VAP TURNOUTS IN PRIMARY AND GENERAL ELECTIONS
IN COMPETITIVE PRIMARY STATES, 1976

State	Est. VAP, November 1976	Primary Election Total votes cast	Primary Election Turn-out, in per-cent	General Election Total votes cast	General Election Turn-out, in per-cent	Difference Between Primary and General Election Turnouts
Alabama	2,501,000	665,855	26.6	1,139,897	45.6	− 19.0
Arkansas	1,503,000	534,341	35.5	762,622	50.7	− 15.2
California	15,294,000	5,709,853	37.3	7,456,917	49.3	− 12.0
Florida	6,326,000	1,910,149	30.2	2,936,679	46.4	− 16.2
Idaho	567,000	164,960	29.1	330,550	58.3	− 29.2
Illinois	7,718,000	2,087,807	27.0	4,562,865	59.1	− 32.1
Indiana	3,640,000	1,245,715	34.2	2,175,780	59.8	− 25.6
Kentucky	2,374,000	439,534	18.5	1,140,377	48.0	− 29.5
Maryland	2,863,000	757,717	26.5	1,384,598	48.4	− 21.9
Massachusetts	4,173,000	941,950	22.6	2,453,359	58.8	− 36.2
Michigan	6,268,000	1,771,480	28.3	3,579,255	57.1	− 28.8
Montana	518,000	196,620	37.9	316,852	61.2	− 23.3
Nebraska	1,080,000	395,390	36.6	579,888	53.7	− 17.1
Nevada	424,000	122,991	29.0	193,014	45.5	− 16.5
New Hampshire	574,000	187,312	32.6	333,090	58.0	− 25.4
North Carolina	3,847,000	798,559	20.7	1,662,078	43.2	− 22.5
Ohio	7,459,000	2,083,207	27.9	3,992,495	53.5	− 25.6
Oregon	1,653,000	730,167	44.2	969,948	58.7	− 14.5
Rhode Island	648,000	74,700	11.5	389,129	60.0	− 48.5
South Dakota	469,000	142,748	30.4	297,772	63.5	− 33.1
Tennessee	2,958,000	574,359	19.4	1,455,478	49.2	− 29.8
Texas	8,503,000	1,979,001	23.3	3,917,065	46.1	− 22.8
Vermont	327,000	72,270	22.1	176,862	54.1	− 32.0
Wisconsin	3,211,000	1,333,373	41.5	2,040,095	63.5	− 22.0
Mean turnout			28.9		53.3	− 24.4

Source: Data on voting-age population and votes cast in the primaries are from the source cited in Table 3. Votes cast in the 1976 general election are taken from the final summary in *Congressional Quarterly Weekly Report*, November 6, 1976, p. 3118.

half as large as turnout in the ensuing general elections for the same offices.

The figures in Table 5 also show some striking variations in primary–general turnout increase from one state to another. The increase varies from a low of 12 points for California to a high of 48.5

points for Rhode Island. Indeed, knowing a state's turnout in its competitive presidential primary is not a very good basis for predicting its turnout in the ensuing general election: the correlation (r_s) between the states' rankings on primary turnouts and their rankings on general-election turnouts was only .39.

So, while turnout in presidential general elections may be a respectable stream (if not a mighty river), turnout in presidential primaries is a small brook, and in local participatory caucuses it is, as Table 2 shows, a tiny trickle. These disparities among the sizes of the various nominating and electing electorates raise grave questions about the representativeness of the nominators and the likelihood that they will choose the kinds of candidates that are most appealing to the voters. But those are questions that must be answered in other studies.

4. Correlates of Turnout in Presidential Primaries, 1976

Registration Laws. Three recent studies have shown that variations in the states' registration laws explain a good deal of the variance in their voting turnout in presidential *general* elections.[36] It therefore seems appropriate to begin by asking whether registration laws do not also explain much of the variance in VAP turnout in presidential primary elections.

To approach that question, I scored each of the twenty-eight primary states we have been considering according to how many of the five provisions its registration laws have that Rosenstone and Wolfinger regard as the greatest inhibitions against voting in presidential general elections.[37] I found that the four states with only one restrictive law had a mean turnout in their presidential primaries of 29.8 percent, and the nine states with two restrictive laws had a mean turnout of 25.5 percent—so far, according to expectations. But the seven states with three restrictive laws had a mean turnout of 33.5 percent, the highest of all; the seven states with four restrictive laws had a mean turnout of 29.8 percent, the same as the states with only one such law; and Kentucky, the only state with all five restrictive laws, had a turnout of 18.5 percent.

---

[36] See footnote 32.

[37] Information about the registration laws as of 1972 was taken from Rosenstone and Wolfinger, "Effect of Registration Laws," Table 4, pp. 14-15. The main restrictive measures are: registration closed 21 days or more before the election; voting rolls purged every three years or less; registration offices not open in the evening or on Saturdays; registration only at the city level, not at the precinct level; and no absentee registration allowing for registration of the sick, disabled, and absent.

It seems, then, that registration laws do not explain as much about turnout in primary elections as they do about turnout in general elections. This finding should not surprise us unduly, in the light of the fact, noted above, that the correlation (r_x) between the states' VAP turnouts in the 1976 presidential primaries and in the general election was only .39.

Holding the registration factor constant by using the RV base, the figures in Table 3 show that in the twenty-six states on which we have voting *and* registration data, by the time of the 1976 primaries a grand total of 57,709,858 persons had overcome whatever barriers their states' registration laws posed and were eligible to vote in the primaries. Yet only 25,508,673 of these persons actually voted. The mean turnout for the twenty-six states was 42.9 percent of RVs and 28.2 percent of VAP. But the individual state figures in Table 3 show that there were wide variations among the states, and we need to look at a number of correlates to seek explanations for these variations.

Primary Laws. In the course of the general drive in recent years for more participation in presidential nominations, a number of states have amended their presidential primary laws or written new ones incorporating various features that are expected to increase the ease and meaningfulness of voting and therefore the size of turnout. We will examine four of these provisions.

(1) Binding presidential-preference polls. Many law-makers have felt that voters are more likely to vote in primaries if the ballot gives them an opportunity to express their preference for a national presidential candidate directly—rather than indirectly, by voting for a candidate for convention delegate who has expressed a preference for that national candidate. Presidential preference polls have been established for this purpose, and only two of our twenty-six states (Alabama and Texas) have no such poll. Their mean RV turnout was 37.0 percent, compared with a mean turnout of 43.4 percent for the twenty-four states that held preference polls.

But there are preference polls and preference polls. For example, in seven of the states with preference polls (Illinois, Nebraska, New Hampshire, New Jersey, Pennsylvania, Vermont, and West Virginia) the poll is not binding upon the delegates, but is only advisory—a "beauty contest," some journalists call it. In these states the mean turnout was 41.0 percent.

In three states (Georgia, Maryland, and Montana) the preference poll's results are binding on the delegates of one party but not the other; their mean turnout was 42.0 percent.

The remaining fourteen states adopted what is presumably the participatory deal: the results of the preference polls are binding on all the delegates of both parties. These states had a mean turnout of 44.9 percent. In short, though the differences in mean turnouts among these groups of states were small, they did proceed in a linear fashion: the more closely the presidential preference poll approached the ideal of binding the delegates, the higher—by a small margin—was the turnout.

(2) *Proportionality.* The Democratic party's post-1972 Commission on Delegate Selection and Party Structure, or Mikulski commission, adopted several rules intended to improve the states' presidential primary laws. One of the most radical changes from the past was decreed by Rule 11, which required that each state's delegates be allocated in proportion to the popular votes cast for presidential aspirants:

> At all stages of the delegate selection process, delegations shall be allocated in a fashion that fairly reflects the expressed preference of the primary voters . . . except that preferences securing less than 15 percent of the votes cast for the delegation need not be awarded any delegates.[38]

However, in a later ruling the Democratic National Committee allowed an exception to this requirement: the committee held that if a state so desires, it can adopt a winner-take-all system for delegates selected at the congressional district level—a system that soon came to be labeled the loophole primary, since it was presumably a way of escaping from the full rigors of strict proportionality.[39]

Perhaps the main argument in favor of proportionality was that of justice—justice to the candidates in that they would get the full benefit of their popular support, and justice to the voters in that the vote of each would count in selecting some delegates and few voters' votes would be wasted (by being cast for candidates who received no delegates). But a strong secondary argument was that voters would be more inclined to vote in a primary where their votes would not be wasted than in a winner-take-all statewide primary or even in a loophole primary with a winner-take-all system at the congressional-district level.

This latter argument receives little support from the actual turnout figures. Of our twenty-six states, twelve required proportionality for both parties, and they had a mean turnout of 42.6 percent. Ten

[38] *Democrats All,* p. 18.
[39] See *Congressional Quarterly Weekly Report,* August 16, 1975, p. 1812.

had loophole primaries for both parties, and their mean turnout was 40.9 percent. Four states required proportionality for the Democrats but not for the Republicans; their mean turnout was 47.9 percent, but that figure was heavily influenced by the inclusion of California, which, with 74.1 percent, had the highest RV turnout of all the states. If we omit California, the mean turnout of the three other states in this group was 39.2 percent. It seems, then, that there was only a small relationship between the extent of proportionality and primary turnout.

(3) *Blanket ballot versus volunteer ballot.* A paper by William D. Morris and Otto A. Davis reported that in pre-1976 presidential primaries turnout was increased by the use of the Oregon-style "blanket ballot." [40] This is a system in which state officials determine who are each party's serious presidential contenders and put them on the preference poll ballot without any action by the contenders. Indeed, persons placed on the ballot in this manner can have their names removed only by filing affidavits that they are not candidates for the presidency (an action that, among other things, makes them ineligible for federal campaign funds).

As we have already seen, two of our twenty-six states did not have a presidential preference poll of any kind. Of the remaining twenty-four, fourteen used the blanket ballot, and they had a mean RV turnout of 44.5 percent. The other ten used the "volunteer ballot" system, in which contenders have their names placed on the preference poll only if they or their supporters petition to do so. If they take no initiative, the contender's name will not be on the ballot. These ten states had a mean turnout of 41.8 percent. The turnout differences are small, but they do correspond with the Morris-Davis finding, so the blanket ballot may indeed have some small relationship with increased turnout.

(4) *Closed versus crossover primaries.* The Mikulski commission's Rule 2-A required that "State Parties must take all feasible steps to restrict participation in the delegate selection process to Democratic voters only." [41] The object, of course, was to prevent Republicans from participating in the selection of Democratic presidential nominees. But, as we noted earlier, the various state primary laws have provided two very different ways of accomplishing this objective. One is the closed primary, in which the voter must register his party preference well in advance of primary day to be eligible to

---

[40] Morris and Davis, "Sport of Kings."
[41] *Democrats All*, Rule 2-A.

vote in the primary of the party he prefers. The other is the cross-over primary, in which the voter can choose on primary day to vote in whatever party's primary he wishes.

It is often argued that the crossover primary encourages greater participation, since the voter is freer to vote in the party contest that interests him most at the time of voting and does not restrict him to a party choice made weeks or months earlier. This seems plausible enough, but the data show just the opposite—and by one of the widest margins encountered in this entire study. The closed-primary states had a mean turnout of 50.9 percent, while the crossover states had a mean turnout of only 34.9 percent.

This difference is so large and so contrary to the expectations of advocates of crossover primaries that it seems reasonable to ask whether it is a truly independent relationship or merely a reflection of other factors. I sought to answer this question by controlling for the only other two factors that produce comparably large differences in turnout—educational level of the states' populations and levels of primary-campaign spending. The results are summarized in Table 6.

The figures in Table 6 show clearly that controlling for education or campaign spending does not weaken the differences in turnout between closed and crossover primaries at all. Within each of the four groups of states—higher education, lower education, higher campaign spending, lower campaign spending—the closed-primary states had substantially higher mean levels of turnout than the cross-over states. *Why* this should be so is an intriguing question far too complicated to be considered here; but the fact that it *is* so might well give those who write the states' primary laws something to think about.

To summarize: the data presented above make it clear that variations in the primary rules did affect turnout somewhat. The states with presidential preference polls had a somewhat higher mean turnout than those with none; those with binding preference polls had a slightly higher mean turnout than those with non-binding polls; those with some proportionality had a slightly higher mean turnout than those with loophole primaries; and those with blanket ballots had slightly higher mean turnout than those with volunteer ballots. All these differences were modest, and in the direction of the participatory reformers' expectations. But by far the greatest difference was in the *opposite* direction: the states with closed primaries had a substantially higher mean turnout than the states with crossover primaries. So the rules made some difference but hardly *the* difference. We turn now to other correlates.

Table 6

PRIMARY VOTING TURNOUT RELATED TO OPENNESS OF PRIMARY, BY EDUCATIONAL LEVEL AND BY CAMPAIGN SPENDING

Educational Level

States with above median proportions of population with more than 8 years education				States with below median proportions of population with more than 8 years education			
Closed primaries		Crossover primaries		Closed primaries		crossover primaries	
CA	74.1	ID	36.0	KY	28.4	AL	37.1
FL	56.5	IN	42.8	NC	35.2	AR	55.6
MA	53.3	MI	38.7	PA	43.5	GA	33.0
MD	45.1	MT	47.8	SD	38.9	IL	36.3
NE	53.7	VT	27.1	WV	50.7	NJ	17.2
NH	58.6					RI	14.5
NV	62.1					TN	30.2
OR	62.0					TX	36.9
Mean:	58.2	Mean:	38.5	Mean:	39.3	Mean:	32.6

Campaign Spending

States with above median primary-campaign spending				States with below median primary-campaign spending			
Closed primaries		Crossover primaries		Closed primaries		Crossover primaries	
CA	74.1	IL	36.3	KY	28.4	AL	37.1
FL	56.5	IN	42.8	PA	43.5	AR	55.6
MA	53.3	TN	30.2	SD	38.9	GA	33.0
MD	45.1	TX	36.9	WV	50.7	ID	36.0
NE	53.7					MI	38.7
NH	58.6					MT	47.8
NV	62.1					NJ	17.2
NC	35.2					RI	14.5
OR	62.0					VT	27.1
Mean:	55.6	Mean:	36.5	Mean:	40.4	Mean:	34.1

Source: Author's calculations. Data on educational level obtained from Bureau of the Census, *Statistical Abstract of the United States, 1974*; for source of data on campaign spending, see footnote 44; for source of turnout data, see Table 3.

Dates of the Primaries. A number of commentators have remarked on the special importance of the early primaries. The candidates who do well in these races are soon established by the news media as the front runners.[42] This happy status enables them to attract still more attention from the media, elevate their standing in the public opinion polls, raise more money, and generally enjoy the advantage of "momentum," which is so important in the early going. This is why New Hampshire, despite the mere handful of convention delegates it elects (less than 1 percent of all delegates) and despite the unrepresentativeness of its population, is important: for a generation it has been the first state to hold a primary in each presidential year.

Accordingly, it seems reasonable to hypothesize that the greater importance of the early primaries will be reflected in higher turnouts. The 1976 data, however, do not confirm this view: the correlation (r_s) between the earliness of primary dates and turnouts is only .16. The listings in Table 3 show that the highest turnout in 1976 came in the California primary, which was held on June 8, the *last* date on which primaries were held. The second and third highest turnouts came in Nevada and Oregon, both of which were held on May 25, the third date from the last.

It could be argued, of course, that the Democratic contest was effectively over after Carter's elimination of Jackson in the Pennsylvania primary of April 27, and this explains why turnouts in the later Democratic primaries declined. Perhaps so—but the Republican experience does not support this explanation. The contest between Ford and Reagan stayed hot right up to the very end, indeed, to the convention itself. Yet when we look at the Republican turnout in the thirteen closed-primary states, the correlation between earliness of the primary date and turnout is $-.13$. Accordingly, whatever the importance of the earlier primaries for momentum, it is not reflected in significantly higher turnouts.

Campaign Spending. The prime objective of a political campaign is to stimulate a candidate's potential voters sufficiently that they will go to the polls on election day and vote for him. In recent years many campaigns, and certainly those for the primary and general elections for the presidency, have come to be managed by highly paid professionals—campaign consultants, public relations experts, advertising and media specialists, pollsters, fund-raisers, and the like.[43]

---

[42] Doing well usually means winning more votes than expected by the news media, not necessarily winning more votes than the other candidates.

[43] These and related matters are discussed in detail in Robert Agranoff, ed., *The New Style in Election Campaigns*, 2d ed. (Boston: Holbrook Press, Inc., 1976).

The new professionalism presumably makes for more effective campaigns, and one might reasonably hypothesize a strong relationship between variations in the money spent in the 1976 presidential primary campaigns and variations in the size of the voting turnouts.

At the time of writing the best data available on campaign spending in the primaries were figures from the Federal Election Commission on the total amount spent in each state by the three leading candidates, Jimmy Carter, Gerald Ford, and Ronald Reagan.[44] Since the candidates were permitted by law to spend larger amounts in larger states, the absolute spending figures are misleading, and we need a standardized measure of campaign spending for purposes of comparing one state with another. Accordingly, in each state I have taken the candidates' reported total actual expenditures as a percentage of their legal limit. Consider Florida, for example:

Candidate	Legal Limit	Actual Expenditures	Percent of Legal Limit
Carter	1,050,851	498,458	47.4
Ford	1,050,851	844,215	80.3
Reagan	1,050,851	790,979	75.3
Total	3,152,553	2,133,652	67.7

Using the total percentage—the actual expenditures of all three candidates as a percentage of their combined legal limit—as the measure of campaign spending in each state's primary, for all twenty-six states the correlation (r_s) between campaign spending and primary turnout of registered voters was .40—one of the strongest relationships we have encountered in this analysis.

It could be argued, however, that the independent variable is misleading because it includes expenditures by Carter but not by any of the other Democratic candidates. To test this objection, I took the data for Ford and Reagan in the thirteen closed-primary states and correlated it with the turnout of registered Republican voters in those states. The correlation (r_s) was .42, only two points higher than that for both parties combined. It therefore appears that campaign spending is one of the factors most strongly associated with primary turnout.

---

[44] The figures are set forth in a memorandum, dated October 19, 1976, to the Federal Election Commission from staffer Robert Pease. I was furnished a copy through the courtesy of Dr. Herbert Alexander, director of the Citizens Research Foundation.

Closeness of the Contests. It seems reasonable to expect a strong relationship between the perceived closeness of the contests in the 1976 presidential primaries and the size of the turnouts. It would seem that the closer the voters expect the contest to be the more they will feel that their votes will significantly affect the outcome; and the more they expect their votes to "count for something" the more likely they are to vote.

Testing this hypothesis would be easier if we had survey data for each of the twenty-six states showing directly how close the voters expected their state's primary would be. Since we do not, we have to get at the voters' expectations indirectly by looking at the actual closeness of the contest when the votes were cast. For this purpose I have borrowed the index of competition developed by William Morris and Otto Davis for their analysis of turnout in presidential primaries.[45] The formula for any given party's primary in a state is:

$$\frac{\text{percent of the leading candidate}}{\text{difference between the percents of the two top candidates}}$$

(1) The two parties combined. Since most of the 1976 primaries were close contests for both parties, for each state I first calculated an index of competition for each of the parties and then averaged the two figures for an overall index of competition for the state. This procedure yielded a wide variety of scores, ranging from a high of 7339 for Michigan to a low of 0065 for New Jersey. Contrary to expectations, however, the correlation between the closeness of the contest and turnout of registered voters was only .09.

(2) The two parties considered separately. Looking at the two parties separately in the thirteen closed-primary states did not materially strengthen the correlation. For the Democrats the correlation was only .02. To illustrate its components: California, which had the highest Democratic turnout of all, 74.1 percent, had a competition index of only 0153 (Brown swept the field against all comers). On the other hand, Nebraska, with the highest competition index, 4311, had a turnout of only 50.7 percent, which ranked it ninth out of the thirteen states.

The Republicans had an overall correlation of $-.04$. California Republicans also had the highest turnout, 77.9 percent, but Reagan's sweep produced a competition index of only 0289. Meanwhile, the Republican primary with the highest index of competition, New Hampshire with 3529, produced a turnout of 63.0 percent, and Ken-

---

[45] Morris and Davis, "Sport of Kings," p. 12.

tucky, with the second highest index of competition, 1273, had the lowest turnout, 28.5 percent. In 1976, then, there was no significant relationship in either party between the closeness of the presidential primary and the proportion of registered voters who voted in that primary.

Demographic Characteristics of the States. There is little of interest to report concerning the relationships between the demographic characteristics of the states and their turnouts in presidential primaries. The only correlations of any significance were those that turn up in all studies of turnout in all kinds of elections. They show strong relationships between high educational levels and high voting turnouts. In this study the correlation between primary turnout and percent of population with thirteen or more years of education was .39, and that between turnout and percent of population with eight years or less of education was $-.51$. The other demographic factors yielded no significant correlations. For example, the correlation between primary turnout and percent of population living in urban areas was .14, and that between turnout and per capita personal income was .22. So, however powerful the demographic characteristics of states may be in explaining their turnouts in general elections, only the education variable explains much of the variance in turnout in primary elections.

5. Conclusion

Early in this study I noted that advocates of the two different ways of increasing popular participation in presidential nominations have both won notable victories since 1968. One group has demanded that the state and local party caucuses and conventions involved in the presidential nominating process be opened up to full participation by all local activists whose enthusiasm for a candidate or a cause makes them want to participate. Most of their demands have been written into the Democratic party's rules and, to a lesser extent, into the Republican party's as well. The result in 1976 was that an estimated 700,000 activists participated in the Democrats' caucuses in the twenty-one nonprimary states. These 700,000 constituted only 2 percent of the voting-age population in those states, but it was undoubtedly a higher proportion than had ever attended caucuses before.

The other groups are not impressed by these figures. They have sought to encourage participation by millions of ordinary voters rather than thousands of activists, and their main device has been the presidential primary. Their greatest success to date came in 1976, when twenty-nine states and the District of Columbia held presidential primaries, with the result that over two-thirds of the delegates to both parties' conventions were either chosen or bound by primaries. In 1976 over 29 million people voted in the primaries. They constituted about 20 percent of the voting-age population. This was not only a higher proportion than had ever participated before, but ten times more people than took part in the participatory caucuses.

The question now becomes: where do we go from here? It seems to me there are four main possibilities:

(1) We can have a moratorium on reforming the nominating process and work with the one we have—much as our forebears did from 1832 to 1904 and from 1920 to 1968.

(2) We can undo some of the recent reforms, perhaps by persuading some states to repeal their presidential primaries (as New Mexico did after 1972) and/or by persuading the parties, particularly the Democrats, to revise their delegate selection rules to give a greater voice to party regulars.

(3) We can make the process even more participatory by encouraging more states to enact presidential primaries.

(4) We can take the final step on the participatory road by having Congress enact some form of a national presidential primary.

Whatever may be the relative desirability of these alternatives, the third and fourth seem to be the waves of the future. Accordingly, this paper, by setting forth the nature and correlates of turnout in the 1976 presidential primaries, has sought to provide some data and other considerations that might help us estimate the consequences of certain rules changes for turnouts in future primaries. On the basis of the preceding analysis, I believe we can make at least the following educated guesses:

First, if we have more state primaries or adopt a national primary, the overall voting turnout at the primaries will certainly be larger in absolute numbers than it was in 1976. As a *proportion* of all potential voters, however, it will be not much more than half of the turnout in the ensuing general elections.

Second, if we confine ourselves to manipulating the rules internal to the primaries themselves, moving from crossover to closed primaries will stimulate turnout by 10 percent or more.

Third, if we also change the laws regulating the environment in which primaries operate, then the adoption of universal registration and a raise in or abolition of the limits on campaign spending will help boost turnout as well.

No matter how many rules we change, however, turnouts in presidential primaries will always be substantially smaller than those in presidential general elections. Whether nominations made by these special primary electorates will achieve the goals claimed for them of more representative conventions, more legitimate nominations, and greater general popular support for our political system is still an open question. All we can say on the basis of what we have learned about 1976 is that they have not yet done so.